CIVIL RIGHTS STORIES

Slavery

Written by Catherine Chambers with illustrations by Toby Newsome

PowerKiDS press.

Published in 2026
by The Rosen Publishing Group, Inc.
2544 Clinton Street, Buffalo, NY 14224

First published in Great Britain in 2021 by
The Watts Publishing Group

Editor: Amy Pimperton
Designer: Peter Scoulding
Cover design: Peter Scoulding
Illustrations: Toby Newsome
Page 2 photograph
© Adenike Oke

Cataloging-in-Publication Data

Names: Chambers, Catherine, author. | Newsome, Toby, illustrator.
Title: Slavery / by Catherine Chambers, illustrated by Toby Newsome.
Description: Buffalo, NY : PowerKids Press, 2026. | Series: Civil rights stories | Includes glossary and index.
Identifiers: ISBN 9781499453799 (pbk.) | ISBN 9781499453805 (library bound) | ISBN 9781499453812 (ebook)
Subjects: LCSH: Slavery--Juvenile literature. | Slave labor--Juvenile literature. | Human trafficking--Juvenile literature. | Forced labor--Juvenile literature. | Slave trade--Juvenile literature.
Classification: LCC HT867.C436 2026 | DDC 306.362--dc23

Manufactured in the United States of America
CPSIA Compliance Information: Batch #CSPK26. For further information contact Rosen Publishing at 1-800-237-9932.

CONTENTS

WHAT IS SLAVERY?

"No one shall be held in slavery or servitude; slavery and the slave trade shall be prohibited in all forms."

United Nations Declaration of Human Rights, 1948

Imagine being bought and sold like a product in a shop. This is what happens to enslaved people. They cannot leave the people who capture or own them and can be taken far from their homes. They work for no reward and are often very badly treated. Slavery began long ago, but continues, illegally, to this day.

There has been slavery for thousands of years. Enslaved people were held captive in ancient Mesopotamia, Egypt, India, Greece, and Rome. Some enslaved people were people who owed debts that they could not pay. Many were taken in warfare. In the time of ancient Rome, entire countries were enslaved as the Roman Empire expanded.

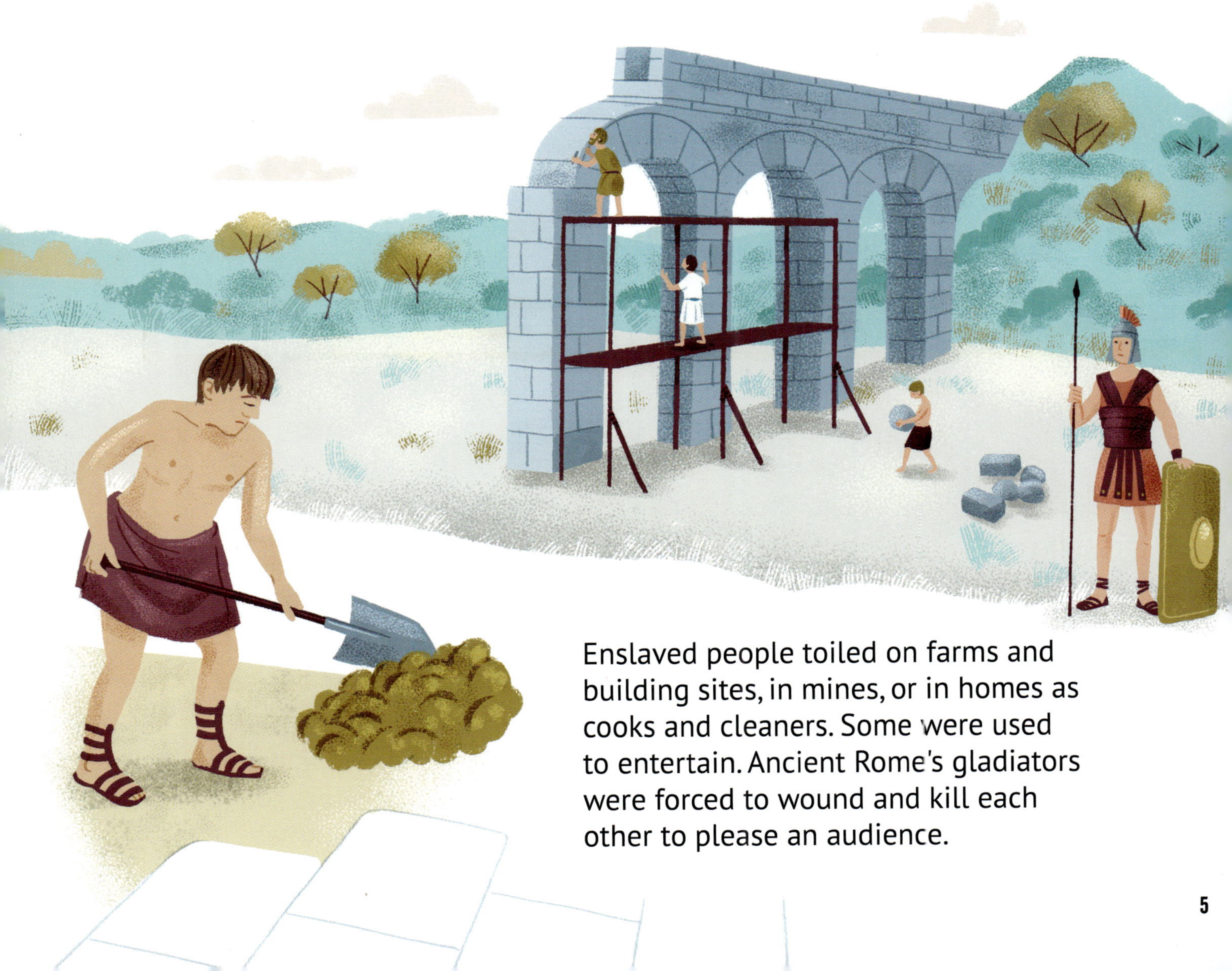

Enslaved people toiled on farms and building sites, in mines, or in homes as cooks and cleaners. Some were used to entertain. Ancient Rome's gladiators were forced to wound and kill each other to please an audience.

SPARTACUS AND FREEDOM

In ancient Rome, some enslaved people worked not only for their enslavers, but also for their freedom. Enslaved people could be freed by their enslavers either after a period of obedient service or by buying their freedom. This was known as manumission.

Other enslaved people, and European serfs (see page 11), earned their freedom by fighting bravely in battle for their lords. Roman gladiators could be freed if they fought and won many times.

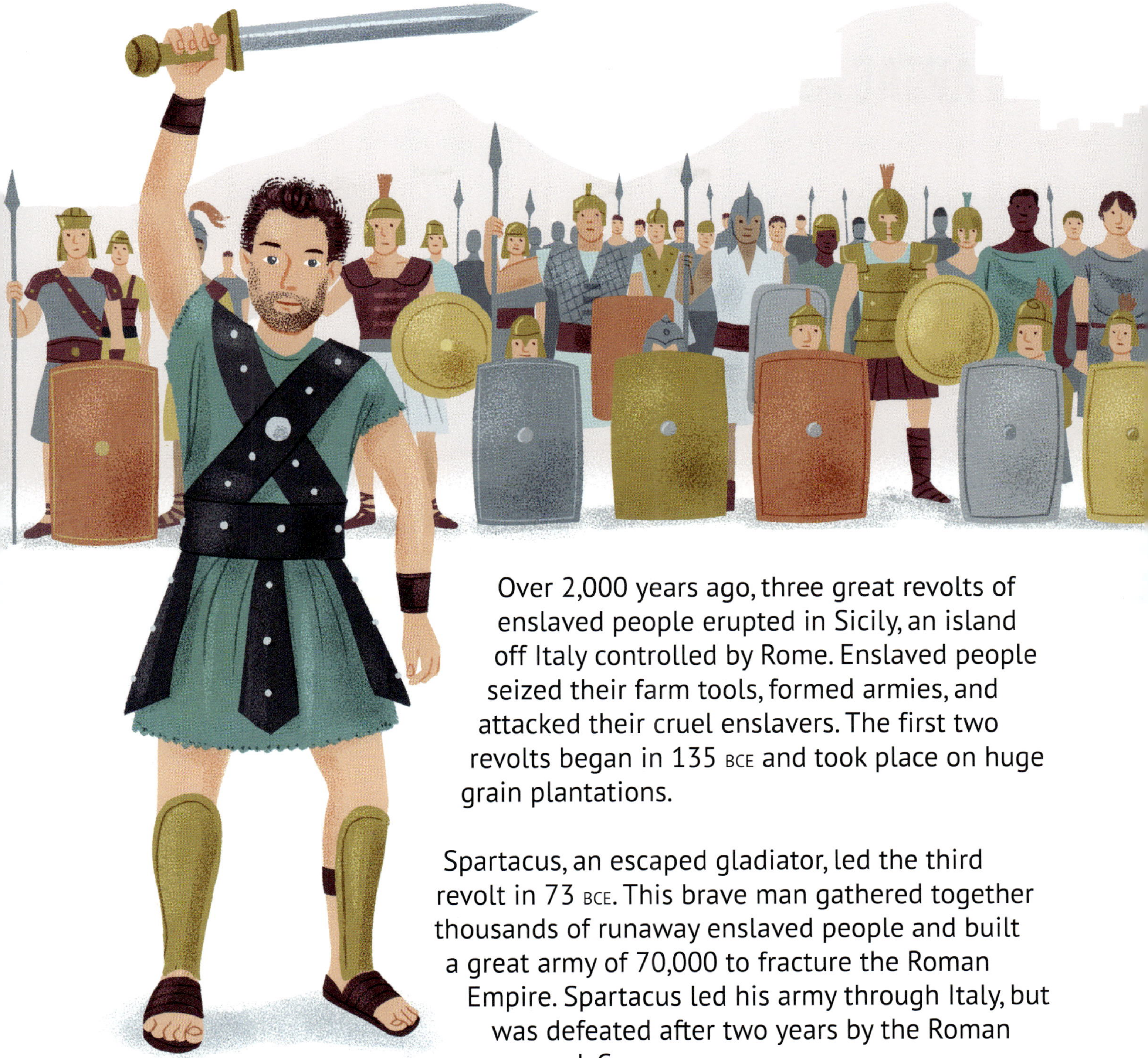

Over 2,000 years ago, three great revolts of enslaved people erupted in Sicily, an island off Italy controlled by Rome. Enslaved people seized their farm tools, formed armies, and attacked their cruel enslavers. The first two revolts began in 135 BCE and took place on huge grain plantations.

Spartacus, an escaped gladiator, led the third revolt in 73 BCE. This brave man gathered together thousands of runaway enslaved people and built a great army of 70,000 to fracture the Roman Empire. Spartacus led his army through Italy, but was defeated after two years by the Roman general, Crassus.

SLAVERY ALONG THE SILK ROAD

Between 130 BCE and the middle of the 15th century CE, countless enslaved people loaded and carried goods along the trade networks known as the Silk Road. These networks were thousands of miles long and ran from China to Africa and Southern Europe.

Enslaved people helped to transport goods, such as silk, tea, porcelain, spices, dyes, and precious stones, from China to Europe. From Europe to China, the goods included woolen cloth, furs, glass, weapons, camels, and horses. The enslaved people were themselves treated as goods to be bought and sold along the trade routes.

Conditions along the Silk Road were harsh and the enslaved people's work was very tough. They endured blistering desert sands and chilling mountain winds without decent clothing or shelter to protect them. They faced wild animals, bandits, and pirates.

Many enslaved people were taken thousands of miles from their homes. Their stories are told in ancient texts and shown in art and architecture.

RAIDING AND ENSLAVING

Many people suffered from slavery in Western Europe too. From about the year 793, Viking invaders captured people across Europe, from Germany in the east to Great Britain in the west. Vikings named their enslaved people "thralls." Today we use the word "enthrall" to mean being captured by something fascinating, not something cruel.

Slavery was just one kind of forced labor in Europe during the Middle Ages (5th to 15th centuries). Wealthy landlords controlled the lives of the poorest peasants, who they called serfs rather than enslaved people. Serfs grew some crops for themselves, but most crops were taken by the lord in exchange for somewhere to live. If a lord needed to raise an army, his serfs were made to fight for him.

After the Middle Ages, in the 17th century, landlords in Russia were allowed to own serfs. Millions of serfs were made to work across this vast land on farms and in mines and factories.

MILLIONS OF ENSLAVED PEOPLE

In 1492, Christopher Columbus sailed across the Atlantic. His arrival in the Bahamas opened up Caribbean islands and the Americas to European traders. For a short while, the islands' peoples welcomed them. But soon, Europeans used their powerful weapons to snatch these lands for their own gain, using enslaved people to work for them.

Over nearly 400 years, enslaved people here toiled on sugar, tobacco, cotton, and coffee plantations or in plantation owners' grand houses. Britain, Denmark, France, the Netherlands, Portugal, and Spain enslaved the islands' peoples and millions from Africa. These enslaved people endured constant brutal treatment.

Millions of African people were captured and enslaved during wars in Africa. Some European nations encouraged and took advantage of these wars. Men, women, and children were chained together and marched to the coast.

From there, ships transported them across the Atlantic, packed under the decks in filthy conditions. Many died of disease and hunger. Those who died or were murdered, along with the weak and sick, were thrown into the sea.

The Atlantic Slave Trade was the biggest system of slavery in the world. It made many people and countries rich and powerful. The influence it had on trade, governments, and people's lives can still be felt and seen today.

TORN APART

Africans forced into slavery were torn away from their families and their cultures. Many were taken to markets of enslaved people in Southern Europe or Africa, and then on to the Caribbean and the Americas. In these markets, children were separated from their parents and families were ripped apart.

Eyewitness accounts describe the horrors of slavery. One of the most famous was written by Olaudah Equiano in 1789. Olaudah was captured in West Africa and was sold first in Barbados, and then Virginia. Olaudah eventually managed to buy his freedom. He became an active and famous abolitionist.

He published his terrible experiences in Britain, the largest nation that enslaved people. Here, a few wealthy and powerful men and women used Olaudah's account to persuade the British Parliament to abolish, or end, the trade of enslaved people.

In his book, *The Interesting Narrative of the Life of Olaudah Equiano*, Olaudah described his horrific sea journey, and how enslaved people were inspected and sold like market goods when they landed. On the island of Saint Kitts, in the Caribbean, he revealed how the name of an enslaved person's new owner was branded on their skin with a hot iron.

FIGHTING BACK

From the start, enslaved Africans fought hard against their captors and owners. Some enslaved people tried to break the chains that bound them during transportation. Others escaped plantations. Rebellious enslaved people worked slowly, broke equipment, or set fire to buildings in protest. Sometimes they organized uprisings.

The Stono River Rebellion took place on September 9, 1739, near the Stono River in the state of South Carolina. A small group of enslaved people, which grew to 60, grabbed firearms from a store and headed south, probably towards Florida. In Florida, the Spanish were in control and were offering runaway enslaved people their freedom.

The rebel enslaved people fought against the plantation owners. Most of the rebels and 20 plantation owners were killed.

After the Stono River Rebellion, new laws made enslaved people's lives even worse, but this did not stop rebellions.

In 1781, south of the United States, on the Caribbean island of Hispaniola, enslaved people rose up against their French enslavers. Led by Boukman Dutty, Toussaint Louverture, and later Jean-Jacques Dessalines, the rebels seized Saint-Domingue, the French colony on the island. At the end of the Haitian Revolution in 1804, they created Haiti, the first country ruled by formerly enslaved people.

Harriet Tubman was one of these guides. She was born into slavery. In 1849, she escaped her brutal enslaver and became an abolitionist, fighting to end slavery. Harriet led about 3,000 other enslaved people to freedom, starting with her own family. She was expert at avoiding those who chased after escaped enslaved people.

From 1861 to 1865 the northern United States states fought the southern states to make them end slavery. Harriet Tubman led soldiers from the north in battle. In one of her many speeches she said:

"Always remember, you have within you the strength, the patience, and the passion to reach for the stars and change the world."
(Harriet Tubman)

HARRIET TUBMAN AND THE UNDERGROUND RAILROAD

The United States abolished importing enslaved people in 1808, though it continued illegally. Slavery continued in the southern states. Enslaved people tried to escape to freedom in the northern states and Canada. The long, dangerous journey was known as the Underground Railroad. Freed enslaved people guided escapees along the route at night from one safe house to another.

HARDSHIP AFTER "FREEDOM"

Enslaved people's stories put pressure on governments to stop the trade of enslaved people. Denmark abolished it in 1803, Britain in 1807, and France in 1848. Yet owning enslaved people and slavery itself was still legal. Britain banned it in 1833. The United States banned it only in 1865. Brazil did the same in 1888. But freed enslaved people and their descendants continued to suffer.

The United States and Britain, along with other nations that had traded enslaved people, were looking to rid their countries of freed enslaved people. Many were encouraged to "return" to Africa, even though many were not born there. As early as 1787, some freed enslaved people were taken to Sierra Leone and Liberia, both in West Africa. Here, they often suffered extreme poverty. Liberia gained independence in 1847, but Sierra Leone became a European colony.

In the United States, Black Americans were often segregated (separated) from white Americans. They were treated cruelly, and given poor education, opportunities, and housing. Segregation in the United States was common until as recently as 1964, when the Civil Rights Act was signed.

Yet even after this, segregation still happened throughout the United States, even though it was against the law.

HUMAN TRAFFICKING

Slavery continues across the globe. The Global Slavery Index shows that there were about 50 million enslaved people in 2021. In 2024, the International Labour Organization estimated that the profits of modern slavery are more than $235 billion a year.

Some people try to escape poverty or war by paying traffickers a lot of money to help them enter richer, safer countries. These traffickers load people onto packed trucks or small boats in order to reach other lands. Many die in deserts, on airless trucks, or on seas along the way.

Other traffickers trick desperate people into traveling to other countries' ports, airports, and stations with the promise of a job. But when they arrive, the traffickers enslave them and take their money and passports so they have no way of escaping.

SLAVERY ALL AROUND US

Today's enslaved people work on cocoa, cotton, and palm oil plantations, or in fruit orchards and hazelnut groves. They toil in mines and handle dangerous chemicals used to make drugs. There are enslaved people all around us on building sites, in nail salons, cafés, and nursing homes. They wash our cars and pick and pack our fruit and vegetables.

Many enslaved people today are forced to work long hours for little or no money. They are often made to live together in crowded and dirty houses, garages, or sheds. They are afraid of going to the police because they have been told that they will be arrested and put into prison.

Some enslaved people are scared of being sent back to war-torn countries. Others fear that their owners will hurt their families back in their home country. Enslaved people's lives are filled with fear.

Not all modern enslaved people come from other countries. Some are enslaved within their own countries and are made to work or to traffic drugs. Many are young, vulnerable, and scared of the gangs that control them.

SLAVERY AT SEA

Fish shimmer in markets all over the world. It is hard to imagine that they are sometimes caught by enslaved people, especially around the Arabian Sea, the Bay of Bengal, and the South China Sea. Enslaved fishermen might not see their homes for years. Some enslaved people are chained on small islands between fishing trips.

A young sculptor, Vannak Anan Prum, was once an enslaved fisherman. He needed money to pay hospital bills for the birth of his first child. So in 2006, he left his village in Cambodia to look for work. He was promised a lot of money to dry fish on land, but soon found himself enslaved on a fishing trawler.

Vannak was allowed only two hours' sleep by night and two by day, and saw shocking violence. He was rescued after five years by LICADHO, a Cambodian human rights organization.

Vannack told his story in a book called *The Dead Eye and the Deep Blue Sea* and in a film about his experiences. Through his book, film, and paintings, Vannack continues to reveal the horrors of modern slavery to the world.

WE CAN ALL HELP

In 1981, the northwest African country of Mauritania became the last to make slavery illegal. Yet slavery continues all over the world. Slavery is hidden. Every day we buy things without knowing if the people who make them are working freely.

Countries and organizations across the world are trying to stop slavery and bad treatment of workers. We, too, can help fight modern slavery by asking questions, such as "Who grows the food we eat?" or "Who makes the clothes we wear?" We can find out about companies' policies on human trafficking and enslaved labor.

In 2008 in Australia, an antislavery organization called A21 was set up. It organizes Walks for Freedom to highlight the plight of modern enslaved people. Since 2019, the walk has taken place in hundreds of cities across the word. Most people walking wear black. Millions of people watch the walk on television and social media. A21's motto is "*Abolish Slavery Everywhere, Forever*."

Marches like this will be needed until slavery has ended across the world.

SLAVERY TIMELINE

Here is a list of moments in history covered in this book that help to tell the story of the fight to end slavery.

3,000 BCE–500 CE: In ancient times, enslaved people were used in many countries and empires. The Roman Empire enslaved entire countries of people and forced other enslaved people to fight as gladiators.

135 BCE: The first of two Roman revolts led by enslaved people on the island of Sicily begins.

130 BCE–1400s CE: Enslaved people toil along the trade routes known as the Silk Road.

73 BCE: Escaped gladiator, Spartacus, leads a third revolt and leads 70,000 enslaved people against the Roman Empire. He is killed in 71 BCE.

400–1400s CE: Serfs in Europe are forced to work for landlords or to fight for them if needed.

c. 793: Vikings begin to enslave many people in Europe as they invade and raid countries.

1492: Christopher Columbus sails to the Bahamas; this marks the beginning of 400 years of slavery in the Americas. Millions of Native American people were enslaved and many died from disease, starvation, and overwork. Millions of African men, women, and children are transported to the Americas, where they are forced into slavery.

1739: The Stono River Rebellion takes place in South Carolina. Most of the rebel enslaved people are killed.

1787: Some countries begin to force freed enslaved people to move to Africa.

1789: Olaudah Equiano is sold into slavery. He later buys his freedom, writes a book about his experiences, and becomes a fierce abolitionist.

1791-1804: Toussaint Louverture and Jean-Jacques Dessalines lead enslaved people in a revolt on the Caribbean island of Hispaniola.

1800s: The Underground Railroad begins operating.

1803: Denmark abolishes the trade of enslaved people.

1807: Britain abolishes the trade of enslaved people.

1808: The United States abolishes the importation of enslaved people.

1833: Britain abolishes slavery.

1848: France abolishes the trade of enslaved people.

1849: Harriet Tubman escapes from slavery. She works along the Underground Railroad.

1865: The United States abolishes slavery. Black people are segregated from white people.

1888: Brazil abolishes slavery.

1964: The U.S. Civil Rights Act is signed.

1981: Mauritania becomes the last country in the world to abolish slavery.

2021: About 50 million people in the world are still enslaved illegally.

GLOSSARY

abolish to formally end (in law)

abolitionist a person who fights for and/or believes that slavery should be banned

ancient Rome an ancient civilization that existed between 753 BCE and 476 CE and was controlled from Rome in what is now Italy

branded to be permanently marked with a a red-hot piece of metal

Caribbean the Caribbean Sea and all its islands; it lies between North America, Central America, and South America

colony a country (or part of a country) that is controlled by another country

combats fights; battles

deck a floor on a ship

fracture to break; when an organization is split up

gladiator a person enslaved in ancient Rome who fought other gladiators or wild animals to entertain free Romans

illegal against the law

landlord someone who owns and rents out land or buildings

Mesopotamia an ancient civilization that existed in part of what is now Iraq

obedient someone who obeys orders or requests

plantation a large farm where crops are grown

porcelain very fine ceramics, also known as china

revolt to take action (often violent) against a ruler or enslaver

segregate to separate people on the basis of their skin color

serf a person who was forced to work on the land

Silk Road the network of trade routes that linked China to Africa and Southern Europe. It was not one road, rather many routes.

toil to work very hard and for a long period of time

trawler a fishing boat that uses large nets to catch sea creatures

Underground Railroad the name given to a network of routes from the southern United States to the north and Canada. There were no actual trains, railway lines, or tunnels. "Station masters" worked along the route guiding enslaved people to freedom, usually at night. Many were formerly enslaved people

Vikings seafaring pirates and traders who came from parts of Scandinavia (especially Denmark, Sweden, and Norway)

BOOKS TO READ

***Black Stories Matter* (series)**
by J. P. Miller and illustrated by Chellie Caroll
(Franklin Watts, 2020)

Children in Our World: Rights and Equality
by Marie Murray and illustrated by Hanane Kai
(Wayland, 2021)

I'm a Global Citizen: Human Rights
by Alice Harman and illustrated by David Broadbent
(Franklin Watts, 2020)

When We Say Black Lives Matter
by Maxine Beneba Clarke
(Wren and Rook, 2021)

INDEX